I0762662

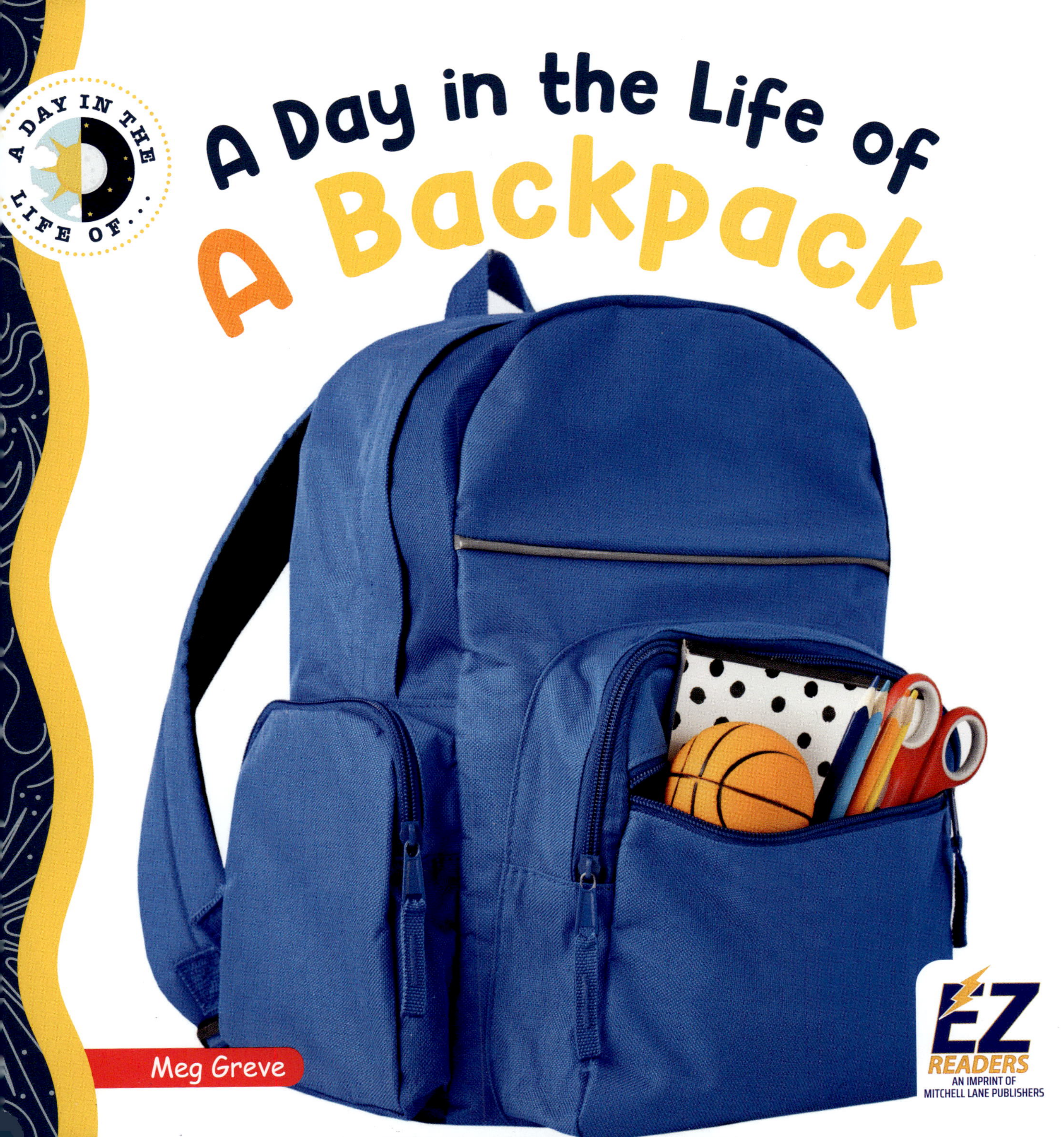
A DAY IN THE LIFE OF...
A Day in the Life of
A Backpack
Meg Greve
EZ
READERS
AN IMPRINT OF
MITCHELL LANE PUBLISHERS

CREATING YOUNG NONFICTION READERS

EZ Readers offer nonfiction for beginning readers in PreK through first grade, using simple language, clear illustrations, and engaging facts to build vocabulary and confidence.

TIPS FOR READING NONFICTION WITH BEGINNING READERS

Talk about Nonfiction

Begin by explaining that nonfiction books give us information that is true. The book will be organized around a specific topic or idea, and we may learn new facts through reading.

Look at the Parts

Most nonfiction books have helpful features. Our *EZ Readers* include color photographs and graphic aids, a table of contents, a glossary, and an index. Share the purpose of these features with your reader.

Color Photos and Graphic Aids

A lot of information can be found by "reading" photos, charts, maps, and other graphic aids found within nonfiction texts. Help your reader learn more about the different ways information can be displayed.

Table of Contents

Located at the front of the book, this list shows the big ideas within the text and the page numbers where they can be found.

Glossary

Located at the back of the book, the glossary defines key words and phrases that are related to the topic. These words and phrases can be found in the text in colored type.

Index

Located at the back of the book, an index is an alphabetical list of topics and the page numbers where they can be found.

With a little help and guidance about reading nonfiction, you can feel good about introducing a young reader to the world of *EZ Readers* nonfiction books.

EZ Readers is an imprint of:

Mitchell Lane
PUBLISHERS
2001 SW 31st Avenue
Hallandale, FL 33009
mitchelllanepub.com

First Edition, 2027.

Author: Meg Greve
Designer: Rhea Magaro
Editor: Kim Thompson

Library of Congress Cataloging-in-Publication Data
Title: A Day in the Life of a Backpack / by Meg Greve

Description: Hallandale, FL :
Mitchell Lane Publishers, [2027]

Identifiers:
ISBN 979-8-89260-842-8 (library bound)
ISBN 979-8-89260-932-6 (eBook)

Library of Congress Control Number: 2025951244

PHOTO CREDITS
Dreamstime: Monkey Business Images,17; Shutterstock: NYS,1; Viktorija Reuta, 1; Alliance Images, 5, 22; Mega Pixel, 5; Pixel-Shot, 7; Yuganov Konstantin, 8, 22; Ted Odeh, 10, 22; Monkey Business Images, 13; Krakenimages.com, 14, 22; LightField Studios, 18, 22; Pixel-Shot, 21, 22.

Table of Contents

I Am a Backpack

I carry your things.

I have a **zipper**.

I have **straps**.

BY THE WAY...
I like to wear charms. They help me dress up!

Good morning!

Homework is in. All done!

Lunch box goes in. Yum!

I keep it all in one spot.

BY THE WAY...
Are you in a hurry?
Do not forget me!

Arms go through.

I ride safely on your back.

I bounce all the way to school!

BY THE WAY...

Please hang me on a **hook**. I do not like the floor. I might get stepped on!

This is my place at school.

I “hang out” with my backpack friends.

(See? I made a joke!)

Time for lunch!

Take your lunch box out.

Put it back when you are done.

BY THE WAY...

Please throw your banana peel away. I do not like to be smelly!

Are those important **papers**?

Put them in.

I will keep them safe.

The bell rings.

Time to go home. Yay!

BY THE WAY...
Show papers to your mom and dad.

It is time to empty me.

Your lunch box goes in the kitchen.

Your homework is ready to do.

Homework is done. Good job!

I make sure it does not get lost.

Set me by the door.

Good night!

BY THE WAY...
See you tomorrow!
WELCOM

Glossary

arms (ahrmz) the body parts between your shoulders and hands

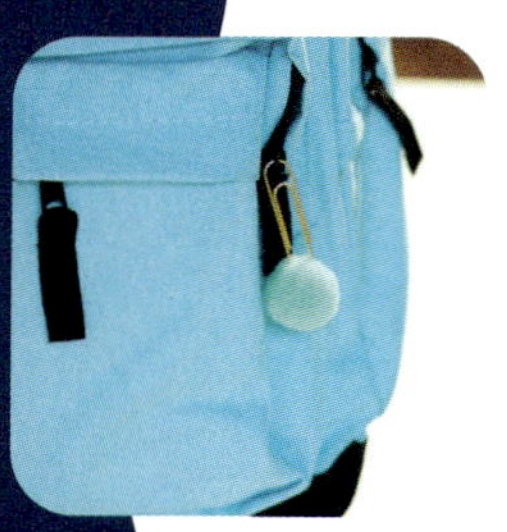

charms (chahrmz) small objects that are used for decoration and that may hang from a chain

homework (HOME-wurk) schoolwork that students do at home

hook (huk) a curved piece of metal or plastic that you can hang things on

lunch box (luhnch boks) a box that carries food so you can eat away from home

papers (PAY-purz) sheets of material with writing on them; important papers might be notes from your teacher

straps (straps) strips of material that let you carry or hold on to something

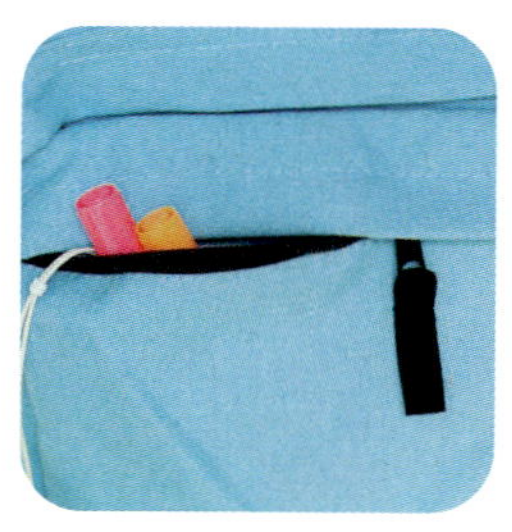

zipper (ZIP-ur) a fastener with two strips of metal or plastic teeth that lock together

Quiz Me

1. I hang my backpack up at school.

   A. Yes B. No

2. I put important school papers in my backpack.

   A. Yes B. No

3. I clear trash out of my backpack.

   A. Yes B. No

4. I remember to take my backpack to and from school.

   A. Yes B. No

ANSWER KEY:

How many times did you answer yes?

4: Awesome! You are organized and ready to go.

3: Great! You are a good backpack owner.

2: That's okay! Keep learning and practicing.

1: You're starting to learn. Keep trying!

Further Reading

Rich, Simon. *Back to School, Backpack!* Little, Brown Books for Young Readers, 2023.

Shearer, Clea, and Joanna Teplin. *Let's Put That Away! My First Book of Organizing.* Random House Books for Young Readers, 2024.

On the Internet

Deep Roots Learning Solutions: Eight Realistic Ways to Avoid a Messy Backpack

readingwritingtutor.com/8-realistic-ways-avoid-messy-backpack

Learn tips for using your backpack well.

Muffin Chanel: How to Make Beaded Bag Charms and Keychains

muffinchanel.com/2025/05/how-to-make-beaded-bag-charms-and-keychains

Find out how to make decorations for your backpack.

Index

About the Author

Meg Greve has been in education for more than 30 years. She is a mom of two kids who used to leave their backpacks on the floor, under their beds, and in their lockers. Luckily, their backpacks were always found and eventually hung up!